Political Constant

Thesis for immutable social structure.

R. S. Chanchhad (Rancho)
Author

Table of Contents

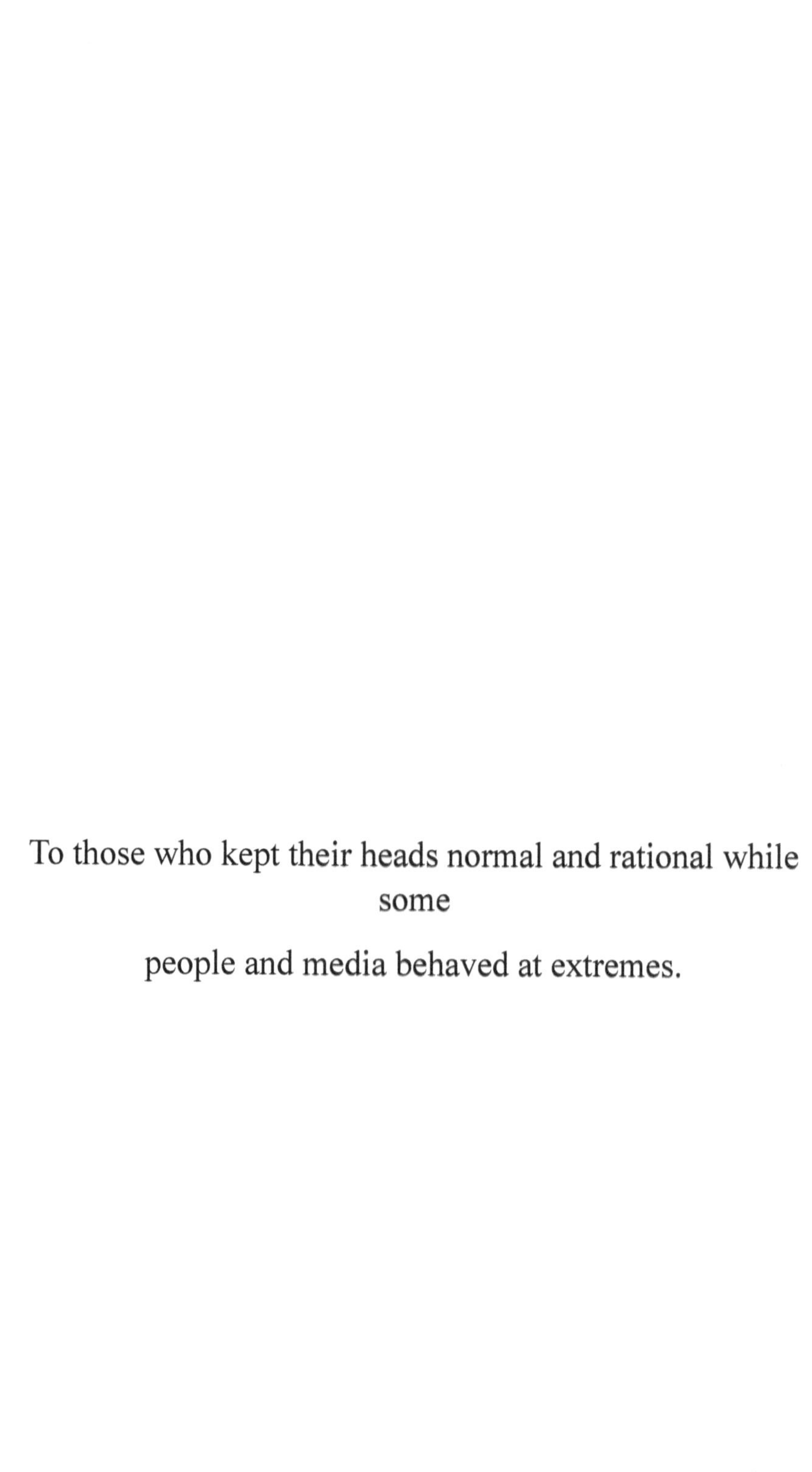

To those who kept their heads normal and rational while some

people and media behaved at extremes.

Prologue

When reading this, think of it like a mind map of concepts. You don't have to agree with all of this to get something out of it.

Chapter 1 is the overview of the ideas.

Chapter 2, 3 and 4 are timeless constituentes separating culture and community. One issue at a time.

Chapter 5 focuses on proposed way of life and solutions to issues we face.

If you're extremely biased towards either side (left or right) of politics, it's highly likely that you'd say that the book is biased towards – liberal values.

Some may find that this is book is alternate angle to economic-left and economic-right, which in a way, it is. But more broad based.

If you find yourself on not on extreme spectrum, but somewhere in the middle of either (left or right) side of politics, then you may agree with some portions but may not necessarily align with solutions.

And if you're coming from another school of thought, you will like mental maps described; but not necessarily the entire content. It's a moderate view, but moderate in the sense which will be cleared further in chapter 1 of the book.

Nonetheless I believe there's enough flexibility in this do-it-yourself model of the changed world order to make this political, financial and economic state of the situations your own.

What I've written is from heart. However, it is very possible that some of the topics and ideas are already existing somewhere over the internet. It's not necessary that everything here is completely new/ never thought before.

I may be not aware of pre-existing ideas. Yet, the collection of my thesis on culture and community is all from best efforts.

But, what exactly is *the problem statement?*

Put simply,

> *Right-wing and left-wing ideologies are either incomplete and/or misunderstood and/or miscommunicated.*

I don't try to over-write anything. Nor you will see anything unnecessary in this book. I've cut the BS out of the way, focusing on delivering valuable insights and trying to write timeless principles.

For the convinience, I have also divided the book into following parts:

- Political Constant in one picture
- Political Constant in a summary

- Political Constant in one thousand words
- Political Constant in maximum detail

What you'll also find is this book is liquid. It's ever-flexible. Unlike traditional book, which is fixed in time, this will keep evolving. You'll find a web version of this on politicalconstant.substack.com which will keep updated.

You will find that existence of both culture and community is interdependent, and justified. One camp doesn't triumph the other.

If there's a unequal weight to one, there will be reversion to mean sooner or later.

Preface

Hey there, reader.

Let me take you on a little journey through the why's and how's of political moderation. Now, why moderation? Isn't politics all about taking sides, about left versus right, about being all in or all out? Well, not quite. Let's break it down.

Why Moderation?

Imagine politics like a ship on the open sea. Too far to the left, and you're in the stormy waters of chaos, where every wave wants to be a revolution but ends up just rocking the boat way too much.

Go too far right, and you're stuck in the ice of tradition, where nothing moves, and innovation freezes over. Moderation is the compass that navigates between these extremes. It's not about not moving; it's about moving wisely.

The Basic Logic

Here's the thing: humans are diverse. We've got different ideas, different dreams, and that's our strength. But this diversity means we've got to find a middle ground where we can all stand without pushing each other off the edge.

1. *Survival of the Fittest:* In the wild marketplace of ideas, moderation wins because it's adaptable. It's not the most extreme idea that survives; it's the one that can live with others. Think of it like tech startups. The ones that make it aren't always the most radical; they're the ones that fit into people's lives without turning everything upside down overnight.

2. *The Social Effect:* A society thrives on connections, on people interacting, trading, sharing. Extreme positions are like firewalls; they block these interactions. Moderation keeps the society open, keeps ideas flowing, and keeps society from fragmenting into isolated islands.

3. *The TIme Test:* History's got this funny habit of showing us that today's radical idea is tomorrow's old news. Moderation takes the long view. It says, "Let's not burn down the house to redecorate." Instead, let's renovate, piece by piece, ensuring the roof doesn't cave in while we're at it.

The Conversational Bit

Now, let us chat about why you would want moderation in your political diet. It is like eating. You do not want just spice or just bland. You want a mix that excites but does not burn you out. Politics is the same. You want progress, sure, but not at the cost of stability.

You've got your culture, right? That is your roots, your identity, what makes you, you. That is often what the right side of politics clings to. Then you have got community, this big, messy, wonderful web of relationships and social bonds, where the left often finds its voice.

Now, imagine if we could balance these. Not erase culture for community, nor stifle community for culture, but find a harmony.

Why This Book?

This book is not here to tell you to stop believing in what you believe. Nah, it is here to say, "Hey, look at the other side without assuming they're the enemy." We are going to explore how moderation is not the boring middle ground but the dynamic dance floor where the best moves in politics happen.

We will look at how moderation: -

- *Keeps the Dialogue Going:* Because when everyone's shouting, no one is listening. Moderation turns down the volume so we can hear each other.

- *Encourages Innovation:* When you are not spending all your energy defending the extreme, you have got space to think, to create, to innovate.

- *Preserves Freedom:* Because in extremes, freedom often gets lost. One side might clamp down on economic freedoms, the other on personal ones.

Moderation seeks a balance where freedoms are maximized. I am going to share how, in this age of extremes, the middle path is not just a safe choice; it is the smart one.

It is where we can all grow, not just survive. And perhaps, we will find that the Political Constant is not about sticking to one place but about moving forward together, at a pace that does not leave anyone behind.

Political Constant in one picture

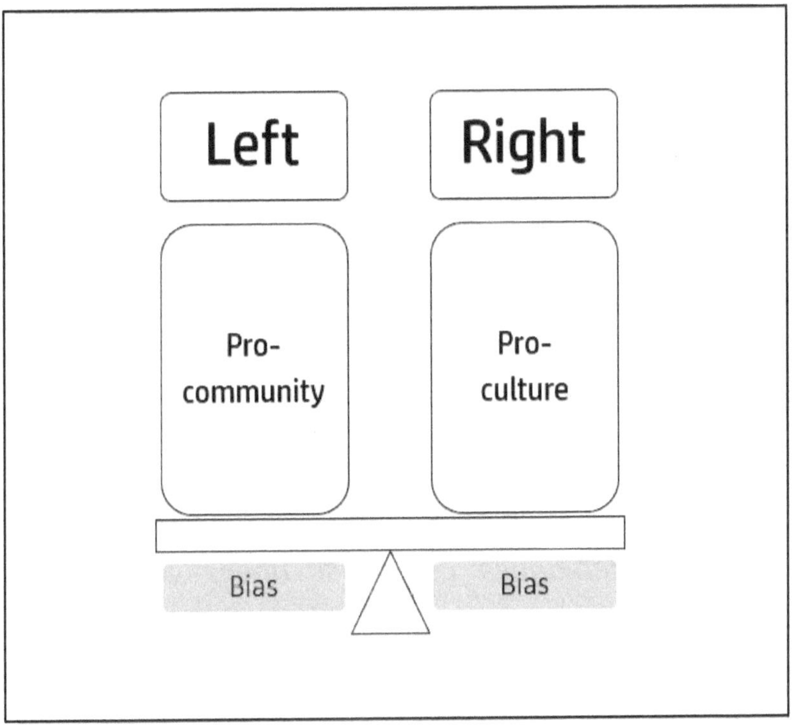

Exhibit 1: Right wing is an ambit of "pro-culture" ideologue and left wing is an ambit of "pro-community" ideologue. Unequal acceptance is bias. Radical means un-acknowledgement of the later ideologue. Moderate means equal balance.

Political Constant in a summary

Right and left; or conservative and liberal – All are wrong way to think about political ideologies. "Pro-culture ideologue" and "Pro-community ideologue" – These are the correct terms. One can-not live without the other. Not accepting even a slight part of the later side is a bias.

Being moderate is complete acceptance of both. Being radical is when the latter is completely un-acknowledged. And both ideologues can exist under capitalism or socialism, anything other than that is just an extreme version of it.

Political Constant in one thousand words

Tip - If you are looking for explanation as to individual parts, hover over individual sentence to get hyperlink to the expansion in detailed version of the book.

Background

As a person, I often feel stretched by extreme right and extreme left biases. I have observed division in people, families, and friends. Not to mention the invisible veil separating people from their government. And government was created *"by people, of the people and for people."*

This is the case for democracies. For socialistic causes, there is no individual-freedom in first hand. The government controls the nation even if nation is operational on an output basis. Between the fight of socialism versus capitalism, geopolitical imbalances have created (and create) hatred, disturbed (and disturb) peace and pose threat to existence.

Tall leaders give hope and direction, common people always drive the country forward and technology accelerates growth. There are always some bad players. However, there is always someone out there who is inclined to moderate and balance the world.

With this background, now I can continue with my Lense of politics.

Thesis

I think left-wing being anti-globalization, pro-Marxist and pro-Leninist having goal of government control is the wrong narrative. Furthermore, the left posing as to achieve egalitarianism or social equality is the also the wrong way to describe what "the left" stands up for. So even if its origin was from set of people who were unorthodox to the political views, religious views and usually disparaging with norms; All the lens through which "the left" has been pointed at, is wrong.

Similarly, the right-wing ideology is often wrongly portrayed as being pro-globalization, anti-Marxist, and anti-Leninist, with the goal of limiting government control and maximizing capitalism. Additionally, the right is often misrepresented as standing up for individualism, free-market capitalism, and social hierarchy, which is an inaccurate depiction of their true goals. The right-wing has historically been associated with those who uphold traditional political, religious, and social norms. Even if it is true, it is a blunder.

In summary, I disagree with the lens through which political wings are described. I do not disagree with any of the values either of the wings uphold. I do not see one over the other.

I propose to see "the left" as "pro-community" and "the right" as "pro-culture."

Pro-Community

Left represents the communal values. These are individual rights of equality. Take examples of voicing individual opinions, equality. Set of values that allow community to be built up. This can happen in socialism (communists), and in capitalism (unions) as well.

Famous communities are Silicon Valley startups, specific demographics (gender, age, ethnicity etc), jobs, labour unions, etc.

Extreme bias towards community leads to more divergence in a society, and misjudgement of history — given extreme bias leads to non-acceptance of cultural values. Take for example, extreme left-wing bias of 2020s, wokeism and resurgence of communism.

If socialism prevails, extremity of communal values leads to communism. If capitalism prevails, extremity leads towards fascism. Both are the two sides of same coin.

Communism is from leader POV, whereas fascism is from unions POV.

Left is basically against accepting historical norms as a rule of thumb. A community stands for a group of individuals with shared values and goals, united by a common purpose or cause. It is a place where people feel a sense of belonging and support, where they can be their authentic selves and contribute to something larger than themselves.

It is highly aligned people with a capacity for collective action that promote individual ideas and rights and eventually gain diplomatic recognition from pre-existing cultures.

Pro-Culture

From a political "right" perspective, cultural values are the foundation upon which communities update. These values are deeply rooted in norms, traditions, and practices that have evolved over time.

The right emphasizes the importance of preserving the established order, maintaining social stability, and respect. The pro-culturist view holds that cultural values are essential for the cohesion and continuity of a society.

In the right-wing perspective, extreme bias towards cultural values can lead to a society that is resistant to change and innovation. For example, orthodox church, amazonian tribes, matured companies failed to evolve, anti-tech establishments, etc.

Saying that societies are held together by shared beliefs, customs, and traditions that are passed down from generation to generation.

Cultural values surround a sense of identity, belonging, and purpose. Pro-culture is not necessarily pro-religion. Religion is a subset of culture, because culture is a medium through which a religion operates. Fundamentally, culture is about respect and stability.

If socialism prevails, extremity of far-right goes to "dictatorship," for example, China under Mao. And if capitalism prevails, extremity goes to "Monarchy," for example, England, France, etc.

Both are the two sides of the same coin.

Conclusion

What I have done is – instead of ascribing a wing what specific ideas it stands for; I have created a broad umbrella under which all things are included. I find this more coherent to accept the other sides. Only culture cannot sustain the earth, nor only community. Both virtues go hand in hand.

You can be anywhere on the spectrum – socialist, capitalist, leftist, rightist, moderate or any other version of your choice. Fundamentally acknowledging community and cultural importance leads to better judgement of political landscape.

Being moderate does not mean zero acceptance of either sides. Being moderate means knowing the importance of both. None of us are living a life solely as pro-culture person or pro-community person. We both have a culture and community because of which we can live.

It has been long established that both are important. Culture will always be about sustenance. And community will always be about multiple individual ideas. Culture will always be bigger than community, and community will always be more in number than culture.

Community becomes a culture in the long run. One cannot escape or triumph over the other.

If we are to live peacefully and sustain humanity, being moderate is the only way forward.

Chapter 1: Idea

What is Right and Left?

Right wing is the pro-culture camp.

Left wing is the pro-community camp.

The political distinction between right-wing and left-wing originated during the French Revolution, where seating arrangements in the National Assembly reflected ideological divides. Today, this divide is often characterized by the right wing's emphasis on culture and the left wing's focus on community.

Right Wing as Pro-Culture:

The right-wing perspective typically values tradition, individual responsibility, and the preservation of cultural heritage. This camp champions policies that reflect a commitment to established social norms, national identity, and often, a free-market economy. They see culture as a vital framework that provides stability, identity, and continuity.

For instance, right-wing politics might support cultural preservation through promoting nationalistic education, traditional family structures, and protecting cultural symbols and practices from perceived dilution or external influences.

Left Wing as Pro-Community:

Conversely, the left wing prioritizes community welfare, social equality, and collective responsibility. Left-leaning ideologies advocate for policies aimed at reducing social inequalities, supporting marginalized groups, and fostering an inclusive society where community resources are shared more equitably.

This includes universal healthcare, progressive taxation, and social justice initiatives.

The left's pro-community stance seeks to build a society where the well-being of the community takes precedence, often challenging traditions that perpetuate inequality.

Understanding Moderation Through Acknowledgment

To delve deeper, let us explore what it means to acknowledge the importance of both community and culture:

Community:

This represents the collective, the shared spaces of social interaction, welfare, and the common good. Advocates for community focus on social justice, equality, and inclusive policies that aim to uplift the whole rather than the individual.

A pro-community stance might involve support for public health care, education, and social safety nets. However, a radical stance would be one that entirely dismisses the significance of cultural identity, potentially advocating for a homogenization that erases individual or group cultural distinctions for the sake of unity.

Culture:

On the other side, culture embodies tradition, heritage, values, and the narratives that give societies their unique identities. Pro-culture positions stress the importance of preserving these elements as they provide continuity, a sense of belonging, and moral frameworks.

However, extremism here would manifest as an absolute refusal to accept any change or integration, potentially leading to xenophobia or an oppressive enforcement of cultural norms that stifle individual freedoms or community advancements.

The Moderate's Balancing Act

The true moderate, therefore, is not necessarily someone who halves their support between these two camps but someone who acknowledges the validity and necessity of both. This acknowledgment creates a dynamic equilibrium:

Recognition of Interdependence:

Culture provides the foundation upon which communities are built, offering identity and tradition. Conversely, a vibrant community ensures that culture evolves rather than stagnates, adapting traditions to modern contexts without losing their essence.

A moderate sees this interplay not as a battleground but as a dance of co-existence and co-evolution.

Policy and Governance:

In governance, this means advocating for policies that might lean towards cultural preservation or community welfare but always with an eye on how one affects the other.

For example, a moderate might support cultural education in schools (pro-culture) but ensure that it is inclusive and promotes community values like tolerance (pro-community).

Dialogue and Compromise:

Being moderate involves fostering dialogue where both cultural preservationists and community advocates can discuss and find common ground. This does not mean both sides always get what they want equally but that each acknowledges the other's concerns as legitimate.

Resisting Extremism:

By acknowledging both, a moderate inherently opposes radicalism. Radicals on either side might view this acknowledgment as betrayal or weakness, but it is a strength.

It is the recognition that absolute positions often lead to conflict or oppression, whether it is cultural hegemony or the dissolution of cultural identities in the name of communal uniformity.

The Societal Benefits of Moderation

Societies that balance cultural integrity with community welfare are more likely to endure through time because they adapt while maintaining a core identity.

Acknowledging both community and culture reduces the risk of societal fissures. When people feel their cultural identities are respected, they are more likely to engage positively within the community.

Conversely, when community welfare is addressed, it prevents the alienation that can erode cultural bonds.

Extreme positions can stifle innovation by either resisting change or changing too radically without regard for established norms. Moderation encourages gradual, considered change those respects both new ideas and old wisdom.

A society where moderation is practiced is equipped with the tools for conflict resolution.

By understanding and valuing both sides, solutions can be crafted that are more integrative and less divisive.

Culture exists for conservation. The community exists for distribution.

What does "being moderate" mean?

Being "moderate" means a person who acknowledges the importance of existence of both community and the culture.

It is the spectrum where absolute zero acknowledgement of the other camp will make you a radical.

In another words, even if you are leaned towards being more pro-culture/ pro-community kind of person, merely acknowledging the importance of the other side makes you moderate.

So being moderate does not mean showing equal support to both ideologues, but acknowledging both camps. And interdependence of both.

Chapter 2: Personal Frame

God

There are about +4,000 religions, faiths, and denominations out there. Us humans and our ancestors have been walking the planet for about +300,000 years. Well, if we have been walking around for +300,00 years, you would think we would have figured out how to get along by now. Have we?

Overview:

The question of God's existence is not a simple factual one with a yes or no answer.

Let us focus on "belief" before God. Because, God is defined in many ways. So for the sake of coherence, I will pick that definition which is most comprehensive.

But it is to be noted that – Belief exists in both the wings. But interpretation and further actions based on belief are different in both cases.

Pro-culture wing has obvious belief in God in religious sense, but also it is not limited to it. There are also those who are pro-culture but not necessarily believe in God.

Cultural beliefs are set of belief which *include* belief in God, but cultural belief is not limited to God.

Culture is essentially a mechanism through which a given religion operates. In that sense, religion is a subset of culture. A given culture can last longer than religion at its core. Why? Because community constantly updates a culture.

In a pro-culture environment, a community is an outlier. Not necessarily in a sense of anti-religion or anti-god sentiment, but in a sense of anti-*norm* sentiment. Community has *belief* in anti-norm values whereas a culture has *belief* in relevance of pre-existing values.

Pro-community wing is a set of people for a cause, not necessarily who are not believe in God. They can have beliefs. It is just so that interpretation and views of a pro-community person would be different than that of a pro-culture person.

It is crucial to understand that there is no such thing as "partial belief." Either there is belief or there no belief. If your belief in certain aspect of a given subject matter, then it is not a complete belief yet it may come under the ambit of belief.

Belief and God both exist and do not exist (depending on individuals) in set of people in both the wings. So as an exercise, find yourself in the following table, as it considers all the possibilities of individuals having their belief systems:

	Pro-culture	Pro-community	Do not know
Believer			
Non-believer			
Do not know			

Exhibit 2: Table of beliefs

If you are a complete moderate, and a believer in God, you will find yourself in both boxes of either columns, but they will be in one row. Because for a moderate to tick on different rows in both columns would lead to contradiction. And bias.

If you are biased towards either side, then you will find yourself ticking only one box.

Note that there is no right or wrong answer here. It is about understanding that is broad and coherent.

It is also wrong to think in terms of logic, here. Belief is internal and does not need reasoning, whereas logic needs reasoning. Logic and belief are two distinct concepts that often intersect but are fundamentally different in their nature and function.

Logic is a *systematic in a sense of reasoning and critical thinking*, based on principles of validity and soundness. It is about deriving conclusions from premises, using rules of inference and deductive or inductive reasoning.

Logic aims to establish the truth or falsity of statements based on evidence, facts, and rational thinking. But rational is not what makes us human.

It is a tool for understanding and navigating the world, and for making sound decisions.

Belief, on the other hand, is the *acceptance of a proposition* or statement as true, often without conclusive evidence.

It is an individual's personal conviction or opinion, often based on faith, intuition, or personal experience. Beliefs can be influenced by cultural, societal, or religious norms, and may not always align with logic or evidence.

From a pro-culture and pro-community perspective, belief in a higher power, such as God, can serve as a unifying force, providing a shared set of values, morals, and principles that guide behaviour and foster community cohesion.

Belief in God can also offer comfort, hope, and a sense of purpose, and can inspire individuals to engage in acts of kindness, compassion, and service to others. However, it is important to recognize that beliefs can vary widely across different cultures and communities, and that no single belief system is inherently superior to others.

What is essential is the respect for diversity of beliefs, and the recognition that all individuals have the right to their own beliefs, if they do not infringe upon the rights of others.

As far as political bias is concerned, the right-wing has risk of weaponizing faith and left-wing has risk of weaponizing compassion.

This is important. And hence belief, God and logic cannot be attributable as "value of that wing" to either wing. All three exist in both.

Pro-culture Narrative:

To explore a "pro-culture" narrative around the subject of God, we see the interplay between culture and personal narratives. These narratives are essential for individual and societal flourishing.

Culture is not a backdrop for human existence but a dynamic force. One that is not explained by logic.

The stories we tell—especially those rooted in traditions—serve as frameworks through which we can interpret our experiences and navigate the complexities of life.

Cultural Narratives as Archetypes:

Archetypes illustrate how religious narratives embody universal truths. These narratives contain individuals with a sense of purpose and belonging, acting as a compass in the moral landscape.

The archetypal figures found in myths and religious stories resonate with the innate psychological structures, guiding behaviour, and decision-making. In other words, parallels are drawn to comprehend what goes around.

Rather than viewing God as a mere theological construct, a pro-culture narrative suggests that the concept of God represents the highest ideal of order and meaning.

In this sense, God is not just a being to be worshipped but a symbol of the values that cultures strive to sustain. This perspective aligns with the assertion that the sustenance of values is preservation of wisdom, as it fosters a profound respect for the complexities of existence and the moral order that sustains society.

Fact remains that individual interpretation of God changes universally. Yet what we see is pro-culture narrative strives for strong belief in values and moral compass.

The Interdependence of Culture and Individual Identity:

Culture and individual identity are deeply intertwined. Pro-culture ideologue is about shaping our understanding of self and community, influencing how we relate to others and the world around us.

Just like communal values, personal responsibility exists strong within the context of cultural identity. Here, individuals engage with their cultural heritage to forge a meaningful identity. This engagement requires acknowledging the values and beliefs that have been passed down through generations, allowing individuals to contribute positively to their communities.

Culture has risk of weaponizing faith and beliefs, and historically it has caused a lot of damage.

Contemporary cultural movements undermine the fundamentals. A healthy culture must balance progress with respect for established norms that have historically provided stability and meaning. Further, community updates any given culture.

This critique is not merely a defines of the past but a call for the renewal of cultural narratives that promote individual and collective well-being.

Conclusion

In summary, a "pro-culture" narrative in the context of views on God emphasize the significance of cultural narratives in shaping individual identity, morality, and community cohesion.

By recognizing the interconnected underpinnings of these narratives, we can appreciate their role in fostering a meaningful existence. Engagement with our cultural heritage critically and constructively, ensures that the values embedded within these narratives continue to guide us toward a more ordered life.

Values are timeless. This side advocates for a respect of values of old traditions as essential for going through the complexities of existence by fostering a sense of connection and purpose.

Pro-community Narrative:

In so far as a "pro-community" narrative is concerned, one can draw from the essence of the significance of community in fostering individual growth and societal stability.

Interconnectedness of individuals within a community and the vital role that shared values and responsibilities play in creating a thriving society.

The Foundation of Community:

Community is not only a collection of individuals; it is a living organism that thrives on mutual support, shared goals, and collective responsibility. Strong communities are built on the foundation of voluntary cooperation, where individuals come together to contribute to a common purpose.

This cooperation is essential for cultivating a sense of belonging and identity, which are crucial for well-being.

A pro-community narrative must emphasize the importance of individual responsibility within the context of community.

True freedom comes with the acceptance of own-responsibility. Individuals here recognize their role in the community and actively participate in its development.

This includes not only fulfilling personal obligations but also engaging in the welfare of others.

By doing so, individuals reinforce the social fabric that binds the community with culture. But it is to be cautioned that communal narrative often weaponizes compassion.

Counteracting Isolation and Alienation:

Communities thrive when they are anchored in shared traditions and values. These traditions serve as a guide for behaviour and decision-making, providing a moral compass that helps individuals navigate the complexities of life.

A pro-community narrative should celebrate these traditions, recognizing their role in fostering unity and continuity across generations.

This is the reason why community keeps updating any given culture, and becomes a culture itself in the long run.

In an age where individualism often leads to isolation, a pro-community narrative must actively counteract feelings of alienation. He emphasizes the need for individuals to engage with their communities, whether through family, local organizations, or civic activities.

By fostering connections and relationships, individuals build a support network that enhances their resilience in the face of life's challenges.

Freedom of Speech

If liberty means anything at all, it means the right to tell people what they do not want to hear. - George Orwell

It is a universal necessity beyond political spectrum. Hence it is unwise to say a political wing stands up for something as essential as freedom of speech.

Freedom of speech stands as a cornerstone of democracy, a principle not just enshrined in legal frameworks like the First Amendment in the United States but also recognized globally as a fundamental human right.

This right transcends political ideologies, serving as a critical mechanism for societal dialogue, growth, and governance.

Whether one leans towards communalistic policies often associated with the left or champions traditional values seen on the right, the importance of free speech remains inviolable.

At its core, democracy thrives on the exchange of ideas. Without the ability to voice opinions, criticize governance, or advocate for change, democracy would be an empty shell.

Both the left and right need this platform to educate, persuade, and mobilize public opinion, ensuring that governance reflects the will of the governed.

It allows for the marketplace of ideas, where the best solutions to societal issues emerge through debate and discussion.

For instance, scientific progress, social reforms, or economic policies often benefit from open critique and dialogue, regardless of whether they come from left-leaning environmentalists or right-leaning economic theorists.

History has shown that when speech is curtailed, often under the guise of protecting public morality or national security, it paves the way for authoritarianism.

For example:

- China's control over information
- Russia's media control
- Myanmar's military coup
- Hungary under Orbán
- Turkey's control over media
- Iran's moral policing
- Venezuela under Chávez and Maduro
- Philippines under Duterte
- North Korea's total control
- … and so on and so forth

Free speech acts as a bulwark against such tendencies by allowing citizens to question, criticize, and resist oppressive policies, a necessity acknowledged by both ends of the political spectrum.

Having an environment where all voices can be heard, societies can better understand diverse perspectives, reducing polarization.

This is particularly vital in today's globalized world, where cultural, ethnic, and ideological diversity is the norm. Encouraging dialogue rather than suppression helps in building a more cohesive society.

In short, free speech does not belong to "a political wing."

Community and Family

It is a choice of consent, culture, and community.

Raising a family is one of the most profound choices two consenting adults can make. This decision, deeply personal and unique to each couple, involves weaving together cultural heritage with communal knowledge.

In this journey, both culture and community play essential roles, shaping not only the upbringing of children but also influencing the future of society itself.

The Choice of Raising a Family

At its heart, deciding to raise a family is an act of consent between two adults. It is a commitment that transcends biological, legal, or social definitions of family, encompassing love, responsibility, and shared vision for life.

This choice reflects their values, aspirations, and often, a desire to blend their individual backgrounds into something new for the next generation.

Cultural knowledge forms the bedrock of a child's identity. This includes:

Traditions:

From festivals and rites of passage to daily customs, these traditions provide children with a sense of belonging and continuity. They learn the stories, songs, and rituals that have been passed down through generations, connecting them to ancestors and history.

Language:

The language spoken at home is not just a tool for communication but a vessel for cultural nuances, humour, and worldview. Preserving and teaching this language can be a powerful way to maintain cultural identity.

Values and Morals:

Cultural teachings often include moral and ethical guidelines, shaping a child's understanding of right and wrong, respect, and the importance of community service or generosity.

By integrating these elements, parents ensure that their children are rooted in a rich heritage, providing them with a strong sense of self within a broader societal context.

While cultural knowledge provides depth, communal knowledge offers breadth:

True Diversity (not woke agendas) and Inclusivity:

Exposure to different cultures, languages, and lifestyles within the community helps children appreciate diversity. This exposure can come from neighbours, schools, or communal gatherings, teaching tolerance, empathy, and cooperation.

Social Skills and Norms:

Children learn how to navigate social interactions, understand societal norms, and develop skills like teamwork and conflict resolution by engaging with their community. This communal learning often happens in less formal settings like playgrounds, sports teams, or community centres.

Global Awareness:

In today's interconnected world, understanding broader socio-political issues, environmental concerns, and global cultures becomes crucial. Community involvement, whether through educational programs or cultural exchanges, broadens children's perspectives.

Shared Responsibility:

The idea of 'it takes a village to raise a child' is not just a saying; it is a practice where community members might play roles in children's education, safety, and socialization, reducing the burden on individual families.

Balancing these influences is where the true art of parenting lies.

Parents should be able to integrate cultural practices with communal experiences... If the objective is moderation. For instance, celebrating cultural holidays while also participating in community-wide events fosters a dual identity that is both rooted and expansive.

Education becomes the bridge between culture and community. Schools, often reflecting community values, can teach about different cultures, promoting an understanding of heritage while preparing children for a global future.

Encouraging open dialogue about both cultural practices and community norms helps children process and question.

This dialogue should include discussing differences, conflicts, and how to respect all identities while maintaining one's own.

Both from within the family and the community, role models illustrate how one can live a balanced life, valuing heritage while contributing to society.

Children need to learn empathy not just for their cultural group but for all humanity. Stories, travel, documentaries, or interactions with diverse community members can foster this empathy.

The Future in Children

Children, through this upbringing, become the bridges to the future:

- Cultural Preservation: They carry forward traditions, languages, and values, ensuring that cultural continuity is maintained, even as societies evolve.

- Innovators and Leaders: With a broad communal knowledge, children are better equipped to think globally, innovate, and lead with a perspective that respects diversity and seeks collaboration.

- Social Change: Understanding both depth and breadth, these individuals are more likely to advocate for change, whether it is societal norms or environmental policies, with an informed stance that considers multiple perspectives.

- Community Builders: They contribute to building stronger, more inclusive communities where cultural identity enhances rather than divides, fostering unity in diversity.

In essence, raising a family with a blend of cultural and communal knowledge is not just about ensuring a child's well-being or success; it is about nurturing individuals who can navigate a complex world with wisdom, empathy, and a strong sense of self.

This approach not only enriches the child's life but also plays a pivotal role in shaping a future where cultural respect and communal collaboration are the norm, not the exception.

 This choice, made by consenting adults, thus has far-reaching implications, influencing not just family life but societal evolution at large.

Distrust in Institutions

In an age where information is abundant yet trust is scarce, the phenomenon of distrust in institutions has become a pervasive issue, transcending political, cultural, and social boundaries. This distrust does not align with a specific political wing but reflects a broader societal shift that impacts how people perceive and interact with established institutions, from government bodies to media outlets, and even beyond into the realms of science, education, and business.

The Roots of Distrust

The seeds of distrust are sown in various grounds. One of the primary reasons is the perceived or real failure of these institutions to serve the common good.

When people feel that institutions prioritize self-interest or political agendas over public welfare, trust naturally erodes.

Scandals, corruption, and the politicization of once-neutral grounds like scientific research or public health guidelines have contributed significantly to this erosion.

For instance, when medical institutions or health organizations appear to align too closely with political narratives, the public's trust in their guidance, even on non-political issues like health advice, wanes.

The Role of Media and Information

The media, traditionally seen as the fourth estate, has not escaped this trust deficit. The rise of digital media, where information is both democratized and weaponized, has led to a scenario where "truth" becomes subjective.

Media outlets, once trusted for their objectivity, are now often criticized for biases, leading to a fragmented media landscape where each outlet serves as an echo chamber for its audience's beliefs.

This fragmentation fuels distrust, as people are increasingly sceptical of any institution that seems to align too closely with any political narrative.

Platforms like X (formerly Twitter) have amplified this issue. Here, information spreads rapidly but with little accountability for accuracy.

Echo chambers, where individuals are exposed primarily to information that reinforces their current opinions, deepen distrust in institutions that might challenge those views.

Social media posts often capture public sentiment, revealing a widespread feeling of alienation from institutions perceived as out of touch or manipulative.

The sentiment here is not about left or right but about a general mistrust in established entities.

The Impact on Different Sectors:

- *Government:* Governments globally are facing trust issues, not just because of policy disagreements but due to perceived inefficiencies, corruption, or overreach. The feeling that governments might prioritize certain groups over the general populace breed's distrust.

- *Business:* Companies, especially large corporations, face scrutiny for their practices, from environmental impact to labour rights. When businesses align too closely with political ideologies or face ethical scandals, it further erodes the thin veneer of trust.

- *Education:* Educational institutions, once bastions of trust, now sometimes find themselves caught in debates over curriculum content, leading to accusations of indoctrination or bias, which alienate segments of the population.

- *Science and Health:* Even science, traditionally above politics, faces skepticism when scientific bodies or health organizations are seen as influenced by political or corporate interests, particularly evident during health crises like pandemics.

This distrust is not just about institutions; it is about a societal shift towards individualism and skepticism of authority. Psychologically, it is linked to a

Economic Views

Freedom of speech, often debated within the confines of political ideologies, transcends these labels when viewed through an economic lens.

It is not just a democratic principle but an economic imperative that fosters innovation, market efficiency, and societal well-being, regardless of whether one leans left or right politically.

Consider the marketplace of ideas, an economic metaphor where speech operates much like goods or services in a free market.

In this marketplace, ideas compete, and the best, most useful, or most appealing ones gain traction. This competition is vital for economic progress, as it allows for the rapid dissemination of new ideas, technologies, or business models.

Without the freedom to express and challenge, innovation would be stifled, akin to a monopolistic market where lack of competition leads to stagnation. Economically, freedom of speech ensures that information flows freely. Information is the currency of the modern economy.

From stock market analyses to consumer reviews, from scientific research to entrepreneurial pitches, the uninhibited exchange of information reduces asymmetries, thereby optimizing market functions.

When speech is curtailed, whether by government censorship or corporate control, it creates an information monopoly, advantaging some while disadvantaging others, which directly impacts economic fairness and efficiency.

Furthermore, freedom of speech underpins the very concept of consumer sovereignty.

In a free market, consumers need information to make informed choices. If speech is limited, consumers might be swayed not by genuine market dynamics but by controlled narratives, which can lead to economic distortions.

This is not about left or right but about the integrity of market transactions. From an entrepreneurial standpoint, freedom of speech is the oxygen for startups and new ventures.

It allows entrepreneurs to challenge established norms, propose new ways of doing things, and pitch innovations without fear of reprisal.

This dynamic not only spurs economic growth but also ensures that economies remain agile, adapting to global changes swiftly.

The tech booms, the rise of social media, or even the sharing economy, all these started as ideas that needed the freedom to be shared, debated, and eventually implemented. Moreover, economically, freedom of speech acts as a check against corruption and inefficiency in government and business.

Whistleblowers, investigative journalism, and public discourse play crucial roles in exposing fraud, waste, or abuse, which directly impacts economic health. Without these freedoms, economic issues could fester unchecked, leading to broader systemic failures.

The economic argument for free speech also extends to its role in education and skill development. An environment where ideas can be freely discussed fosters critical thinking, which is not just a democratic value but an economic one.

Societies that encourage questioning and debate produce citizens who can adapt, innovate, and compete globally. Education systems that suppress speech might produce graduates skilled in memorization but lacking in creativity or problem-solving, attributes essential for economic competitiveness.

However, this does not mean freedom of speech is without challenges or responsibilities. There is the economic cost of misinformation or hate speech, which can lead to social unrest or misguided economic decisions.

Here, the balance lies not in pre-emptive censorship but in fostering media literacy, encouraging counter-speech, and legal frameworks that protect while not stifling speech.

In essence, freedom of speech, when viewed through an economic lens, reveals itself as neither a left nor right issue but a fundamental pillar of economic health.

It ensures markets are informed, consumers are sovereign, innovation thrives, corruption is less likely to flourish, and education remains dynamic.

This perspective underscores that freedom of speech is not just about political expression but about creating the conditions for allowing all economic views.

Chapter 3: Structural Frame

Nature of Wings

These political wings, their ideas are not static. Both wings evolve over time. Often, it baits us into thinking that a given person is changing the political side he or she supports. But that is not the case.

But does that mean they change? No. It is a matter of co-operation among pro-culture and pro-communal values which disguise as dynamism. Both parties dress differently in different events in different time frames.

This is because any given Political Constant is nested with other things that change in different rates.

For community, the vibrancy is much higher and in culture, it is much lower. Why? Because culture is foundationally robust and has core values of sustenance, whereas community thrives on newness and exploration in a sense of anti-norm perspectives.

Another way to think about it is leaves change faster than tree, musical genre changes faster than the medium of music, weather changes faster than the climate, political parties change faster than political structure and so on.

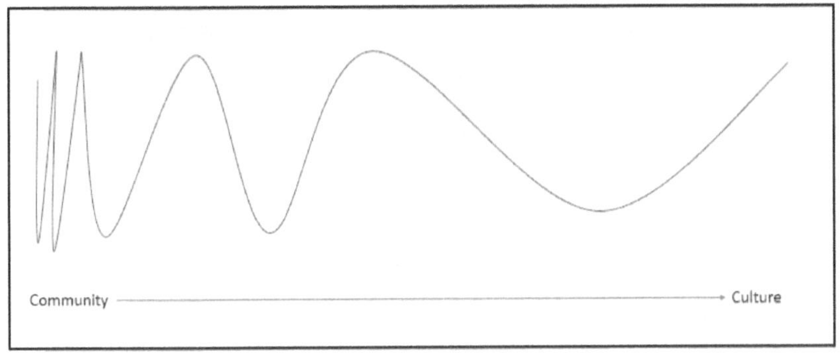

Exhibit 3: Vibrancy of change going from culture to community.

If this was not the way, the culture would have vanished long ago and communities would have failed. Thus stopping human evolution in every possible aspect.

Culture

The concept of the unchanging nature of culture might seem paradoxical at first, given that culture, by its very definition, evolves with the times, reflecting the dynamic interplay between human societies and their environments.

However, when we delve deeper, there is an aspect of culture that could be seen as unchanging or constant, not in its form or expression but in its essence and function within human societies. This essence revolves around the core human experiences and needs that culture addresses: identity, community, values, and continuity.

It is the repository of a group's collective memory, its stories, traditions, and practices that define what it means to be part of that group.

While the specifics of these elements might change—new traditions might emerge, old ones might fade, and values might shift—the underlying need for these elements remains constant.

For instance, the rituals around birth, coming of age, marriage, and death have transformed across centuries and cultures, yet they persist because they address fundamental human experiences. These rituals, regardless of their form, function to mark life's milestones, providing a sense of order, meaning, and belonging.

Moreover, the unchanging nature of culture can be observed in its role as a mechanism for social cohesion and identity formation.

Cultures might adopt new technologies, languages, or customs (as communities update any given culture), *but* the drive to differentiate oneself from other groups, to celebrate uniqueness, or to preserve heritage remains a constant.

This is not about stasis but about the continuity of cultural identity through adaptation. Even in the face of globalization, where cultures intermingle more than ever, there is a noticeable trend towards cultural preservation or revival, suggesting an inherent human desire to hold onto cultural roots, even as they evolve.

The unchanging nature of culture also lies in its capacity to reflect and shape human values. While the values themselves might evolve (e.g., from honour-based to rights-based societies), culture's role in transmitting these values from one generation to another remains consistent.

This transmission ensures that while the content might change, the process of enculturation—learning and internalizing cultural norms—continues unabated.

In essence, while the manifestations of culture are fluid, adapting to new environments, technologies, and societal structures, the fundamental reasons why culture exists—providing identity, fostering community, transmitting values, and ensuring continuity—remain unchanging.

This constancy in purpose amidst change underscores the resilient nature of culture, making it both a mirror to human evolution and a steadfast anchor in the sea of change.

And hence steady, slow but long vibrancy.

And all this is important to note this, while assigning the "cultural" values of so-called "right wing."

Community

Like culture, unchanging nature of community also seems paradoxical in a world where the term "community" itself has evolved to encompass various forms, from traditional geographical neighbourhoods to virtual networks.

However, at its core, the essence of community also remains remarkably constant, rooted in the fundamental human need for connection, belonging, and mutual support.

This essence transcends time, technology, and cultural shifts (where a successful community becomes a part of our culture the culture itself), reflecting a consistent human trait to seek out or create groups where individuals can share experiences, values, or purposes.

Historically, communities were defined by physical proximity, where shared resources, culture, and daily interactions formed the basis of community life. Despite the advent of digital platforms, which have expanded the notion of community beyond physical boundaries, the underlying principles remain: communities are about shared identity, mutual aid, different from culture and collective action.

Whether it is a village in ancient times or a modern online forum, communities live on the exchange of support, information, and various kinds of bonds. The unchanging nature of community lies in its function as a safety net, providing social, emotional, and sometimes economic support.

This aspect has been consistent through the ages, from tribal societies where survival depended on collective effort, to today's urban settings where neighbours or online groups rally around individuals in times of need.

The mechanisms might differ — from physical aid to digital crowdfunding — but the principle of community as a support system remains intact.

Moreover, communities are inherently about identity and belonging. People form or join communities not just for practical reasons but to affirm who they are, to be part of something larger than themselves, which provides a sense of continuity and tradition.

And this connects community and culture. Yet again emphasizing their inter-dependency.

This aspect of community, where individuals find validation and a place to express their cultural, religious, or personal identities, has not changed.

Whether through festivals, rituals, or shared online content, communities continue to be the crucibles where identities are forged and maintained. The unchanging nature of community also reflects in the dynamics of inclusion and exclusion, where boundaries are set, often implicitly, to define who belongs and who does not.

This phenomenon, observed in tribal societies through to modern social media groups, shows that while the tools for communication evolve, the human tendency to form exclusive groups for protection, identity, or purpose remains constant.

In essence, while the forms and expressions of community might adapt to new environments, technologies, and societal structures, the fundamental reasons for their existence—providing identity, fostering belonging, offering support, and ensuring continuity—remain unchanging.

And that's why vibrancy of community is always more, because new expressions keep arising.

This constancy amidst change underscores the resilient nature of human social structures, making community not just a historical or sociological concept but a timeless human necessity.

In the end, this is the nature of wings. This is a resilient human social structure where both wings are dependent on each other. And they are also not against each other. It is just that underlying emphasis of the structure is different.

Falsifiability

I find that there are certain things about both wings of politics which are inherently not provable nor unfalsifiable by nature. Reason for that is they are defined as broad umbrella terms for what each wing stands up for. If any political ideology is a guide/ handbook then this is not the way any GPS/ dictionary should work.

So this is portion is about unfalsifiable elements of both the wings.

Problems are the real assessments. Moderation is the assessment metrics. But political alignments are the handbooks.

Left wing

Left-wing politics typically champions ideals like equality, social justice, and collective responsibility. These ideals are often presented in a way that they cannot be empirically disproven.

For instance, if one argues for wealth redistribution to achieve economic equality, any failure in outcome might be attributed not to the policy itself but to not going far enough, or external factors like opposition from the right or market forces.

This makes the core idea of economic equality through redistribution seemingly unfalsifiable; if it does not work, proponents might claim it was not implemented correctly or extensively enough.

This side also positions itself on a moral high ground, advocating for what "should be" based on principles of fairness or justice.

This moral positioning can make empirical critique challenging because any counter-argument can be framed as a moral failing rather than a practical or factual one.

For example, the idea that healthcare should be a universal right is a moral proposition.

Critics who point out practical issues or inefficiencies in universal healthcare systems might be accused of lacking compassion or being morally corrupt, rather than engaging with their critique on a factual basis.

There are also the critiques of systemic or structural issues within society, like systemic racism or patriarchy.

These concepts are criticized for being unfalsifiable because they are defined in such broad and pervasive terms that any evidence against them (like successful individuals from marginalized groups) can be dismissed as exceptions rather than refutations.

The system's critique is so all-encompassing that it adapts to include any new data as part of the systemic problem, rather than evidence against it.

Identity politics can lead to unfalsifiable claims when policies or positions are defended based on identity rather than empirical outcomes.

If a policy is criticized, supporters might argue that the criticism stems from bias against the identity group the policy aims to help, thereby deflecting any objective analysis of the policy's effectiveness.

Radical left-wing arguments a lot of times engage in what might be called "dialectical warfare," where the debate itself, regardless of its grounding, is used to validate the existence of the issue.

For example, the extensive debate over microaggressions might be used as evidence of their significance, regardless of whether there's empirical evidence supporting the widespread impact of these microaggressions.

There is an argument from psychology that left-wing politics might appeal to certain psychological needs for equality and fairness that are not easily challenged by facts.

If policies fail, the blame might be placed on implementation, opposition, or not going far enough, rather than the idea itself being flawed. This creates a loop where the ideology remains intact regardless of outcomes.

Right wing

These are champions traditional values, which are seen as timeless or rooted in a natural order. So therefore not "necessarily logical" is the usual argument against the right.

These values like the sanctity of marriage being only between a man and a woman or the intrinsic value of a nation's culture, are presented in a way that they cannot be empirically disproven. They can be, given effect on children, society, individual's psyche etc.

But if one argues for or against these values, the debate often shifts from empirical evidence to moral or philosophical grounds, where the "rightness" of these values is asserted rather than proven.

Right-wing economic policies, like tax cuts for the wealthy stimulating economic growth (trickle-down economics), are sometimes criticized as unfalsifiable. Proponents might say that if the expected growth does not occur, it is because the policy was not implemented correctly or fully, or external factors intervened.

This makes the core idea difficult to test definitively.

That is why macro-economic is a large garden and the land is owned by a politician.

Nationalistic sentiments within right-wing politics assert the superiority or uniqueness of one's nation or culture. These ideas are also unfalsifiable because they are often based on subjective interpretations or feelings attached towards history, culture, and/ or national identity.

Any challenge can be dismissed as not understanding the "true" essence of the nation or as external threats or corruption of national identity.

Elements of right-wing populism sometimes involve conspiracy theories (e.g., globalist agendas, cultural Marxism). These theories can be inherently difficult to prove because they often include mechanisms for self-preservation: any evidence against them can be dismissed as part of the conspiracy.

When right-wing politics intertwine with religious beliefs or cultural norms, these beliefs can become not truly provable in political discourse. For instance, arguments against certain social changes (like acceptance of transgender rights) might be based on religious texts or traditional roles, where the debate is not about evidence but belief.

If it were moderation then set of evidences would involve.

Right-wing arguments for strict law enforcement, military strength, or anti-immigration policies often hinge on the fear of loss of security or identity. And they are based on potential future threats or hypothetical scenarios where evidence either way is hard to come by or is interpreted through an ideological lens.

As far as appeal to a negativity bias is concerned, the threats are perceived as more imminent or severe.

This can lead to positions where policies or beliefs are not based on what can be proven to work but on what feels necessary to avoid perceived threats, making these beliefs resistant to falsification.

The unfalsifiable nature of some left-wing political ideas does not necessarily mean these ideas are wrong or right; rather, it points to a challenge in debating and testing these ideas empirically.

This makes left-wing politics more akin to a belief system where faith in certain outcomes (like eventual equality through radical change) is maintained regardless of immediate evidence to the contrary.

However, from another perspective, these ideals are goals or directions towards which society should strive, even if the path is fraught with practical challenges. This dynamic makes the discussion around left-wing politics particularly complex and often contentious.

The unfalsifiable nature here does not mean these positions are inherently wrong or right; rather, it points to the challenge in engaging with them on purely empirical grounds. Which can only happen through moderations.

Right wing ideas are indeed akin to articles of faith or ideological commitments rather than policies or positions open to empirical scrutiny.

Conversely, these principles are based on time-tested wisdom or necessary protective measures for societal stability, which by their nature, transcend simple empirical testing. But again, this is not empirical.

Moderation by "Pro-community x Pro-culture" Definitions

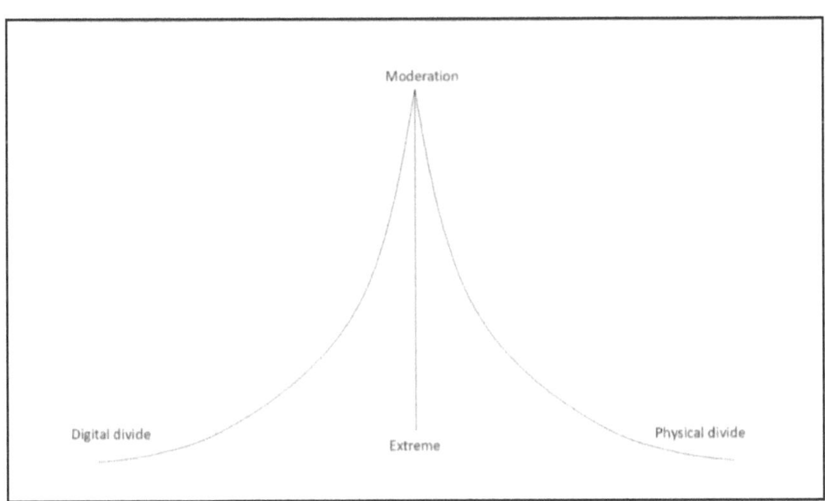

We are at the point where digital divide and physical divide exists both in right, as well as on left. And this has further extended the possible extremes.

Back to *Political Constant*, viewing right-wing politics as "pro-culture" and left-wing politics as "pro-community" can offer a framework that might help in understanding and potentially resolving some aspects of political polarization.

It can be argued that following values are essentially elements of moderation.

Here is how this perspective could contribute to resolving debates:

Acknowledgement of Core Values:

Core values rather than opposition to change for its own sake can lead to more respectful discourse. Motivations can shift debates from adversarial to constructive by focusing on what each side fundamentally values.

Common Ground:

It is the case that both sides are not mutually exclusive but are interdependent.

A strong community often relies on a shared culture, and a vibrant culture thrives in a supportive community. Community updates a given culture in the long time. Culture makes a community make a right decision. A successful community becomes part or the culture itself in the long time.

This realization can lead to policies that integrate cultural preservation with community development, like community programs that also serve to maintain cultural heritage.

Policy Formulation:

When approaching policy, this perspective could encourage solutions that balance cultural integrity with community inclusiveness.

For instance, in decisions over immigration, instead of an all-or-nothing approach, discussions could focus on how immigrants can be integrated in a way that respects and celebrates both their original culture and the host culture, thereby enriching community life.

Reducing Misunderstandings:

Often, political polarization is fuelled by mischaracterizations of the other side's intentions. This is essential problem with extremities, now digital as well as physical.

By framing the right's actions as protecting culture and the left's as enhancing community, it might reduce the demonization of each side.

For example, conservative resistance to rapid changes in social norms could be seen as a defence of cultural identity rather than mere obstructionism.

Empathy:

Both sides are striving towards what they see as a better society, albeit through different lenses.

When people understand that conservatives might fear the loss of cultural identity as much as liberals fear social injustice, it can lead to more empathetic interactions.

Because they are the same things.

However, while this framework can be helpful, it is also important to recognize its limitations.

Not all policies or beliefs will fit neatly into these categories. Additionally, there is a risk of oversimplification, which might ignore other significant aspects of political identity like economic policies, individual rights, etc.

Oversimplification leads to extremes as well. But moderation in any case does not mean alluding to a specific side, but all sides.

Nonetheless, using this lens could be one of many tools to foster understanding and cooperation in politically polarized environments.

Chapter 4: Time Frame

Brief History of How Pro-Culture People Turned into Political Right

The development of political ideologies, particularly those that coalesce into what we now recognize as the political right, can be traced through a complex tapestry of cultural evolution, historical shifts, and societal changes. Here is a simplified timeline and exploration of how cultural evolution might have contributed to the rise of right-wing ideologies:

Pre-Modern Era:

- Tribal Societies: From the earliest human societies, there were always structures of authority and norms. Tribes often had leaders, either chosen through merit, lineage, or strength, reflecting a natural hierarchy that can be seen as a precursor to more formalized political structures.

- Agricultural Revolution (Around 10,000 BCE): The shift from hunter-gatherer lifestyles to agriculture introduced the concept of property, which necessitated laws and governance to protect ownership. This might be seen as an early form of conservatism, where traditions and established norms were crucial for societal stability.

Ancient Civilizations:

- Civilizations like Rome and Greece: These societies developed concepts of citizenship, patriotism, and the rule of law, which emphasized the importance of social order and traditional values. The Roman concept of "Pater Families," where the father held significant authority, can be seen as a cultural foundation for patriarchal values often associated with right-wing politics.

- Feudalism (Medieval Europe): Feudal lords held power over land and people, with a rigid social hierarchy. This system reinforced the idea of hierarchy, tradition, and the divine right of rulers, elements that resonate with some right-wing ideologies emphasizing order and tradition.

Renaissance to Enlightenment (14th to 18th Century):

- Renaissance: With the rediscovery of classical texts, there was a revival interest in humanism and individualism, but it also sparked debates on governance, authority, and the role of tradition versus change.

- Enlightenment: While generally associated with liberal thought, thinkers like Edmund Burke began conservative philosophy, arguing for the importance of tradition, institutions, and organic societal development against revolutionary change.

Industrial Revolution and Beyond (18th to 19th Century):

- Industrialization: This period saw massive social upheaval. While it led to liberal movements advocating for change, it also birthed a conservative backlash. The rapid change threatened traditional ways of life, leading to ideologies that sought to preserve or restore pre-industrial societal structures.

- Nationalism: The 19th century nationalism, often intertwined with conservatism, emphasized cultural identity, language, and history, which are themes that can align with right-wing views on nationhood and cultural preservation.

20th Century:

- World Wars: These conflicts reshaped global politics. The aftermath, especially post-WWII, saw a rise in nationalist movements in various forms, from decolonization to the resurgence of national identity in Europe, often tinged with conservative or right-wing sentiments.

- Cold War: The ideological battle between communism and capitalism further defined right-wing thought, particularly in its staunch anti-communism and defence of free-market capitalism, which became synonymous with conservative ideologies in the West.

- Cultural Movements: The countercultural revolutions of the '60s and '70s, advocating for civil rights, feminism, and anti-war sentiments, inadvertently spurred a conservative reaction. Movements like the Moral Majority in the U.S. emphasized traditional family values, religion, and patriotism, elements core to right-wing platforms.

Late 20th to Early 21st Century:

- Globalization and Identity Politics: Globalization brought cultural integration but also fears of cultural erosion. This led to a rise in identity politics where groups, feeling their cultural identities threatened, often gravitated towards right-wing ideologies that promised to protect or restore cultural purity or national sovereignty.

- Economic Shifts: The shift towards neoliberal economic policies, which included deregulation and globalization, while often supported by the political right, also created economic disparities. This led to populist movements, both left and right, but the right-wing variant emphasized nationalism and economic protectionism.

- Technological Revolution: The internet and social media have amplified every voice, allowing for the rapid spread of ideas. This has both democratized information and allowed for the proliferation of extremist views, including far-right ideologies.

Contemporary Trends:

- Populism: Rising in many democracies, populism often leans right with its emphasis on the 'common man' against an elite or outsider threat, whether it is immigrants, global elites, or perceived cultural invaders.

- Cultural Backlash: Movements like Brexit, the rise of leaders like Donald Trump, or parties like Alternative for Germany (AfD) illustrate a cultural backlash against perceived threats to national identity or sovereignty, often framed in terms of returning to traditional values or making the nation 'great again'.

Conclusion

The evolution of right-wing ideologies is not merely a political phenomenon but deeply interwoven with cultural shifts.

Each era's response to change, be it technological, economic, or social, has contributed to ideologies that prioritize tradition, national identity, and order over radical change or perceived threats to cultural cohesion.

While this narrative simplifies the complex interplay of factors, it underscores how cultural evolution, through its various stages, has continually shaped and reshaped what we understand as right-wing political thought, reflecting societies' ongoing debate between change and continuity, individualism versus collectivism, and local identity against global integration.

Brief History of How Pro-Community People Turned into Political Left

The evolution of communities towards what we now recognize as left-wing ideologies is not a straightforward progression but a complex tapestry woven from historical, social, and economic threads. Here is a simplified overview tracing this evolution:

Early Tribal Societies and Agrarian Communities:

- Prehistoric Times: In early human societies, the concept of community was about survival and kinship. There was not a distinction between left or right, but the seeds of communal living were sown, where cooperation was key for survival.

- Agricultural Revolution (Around 10,000 BCE): With agriculture came the idea of common land, shared labour, and communal decision-making. This could be seen as an early precursor to collective action, albeit for survival rather than political ideology.

Ancient Civilizations and Early Empires:

- Classical Civilizations: Both Greece and Rome had elements that could be seen as proto-leftist, like democratic processes in Athens or the Plebeian struggles for rights in Rome, where community involvement in governance was valued.

- *Medieval Europe:* Feudalism might not seem leftist, but the peasantry's occasional rebellions or the formation of guilds hinted at collective bargaining and community welfare, albeit within a rigid hierarchy.

Renaissance to Enlightenment:

- Renaissance (14th to 17th Century): The resurgence of interest in human dignity and individual rights began challenging divine rights and absolute monarchy, paving the way for ideas like equality and liberty.

- Enlightenment (17th to 18th Century): This era's thinkers like Rousseau with his "social contract" or the American founding fathers advocating for equality, laid intellectual groundwork for communal governance and rights.

Industrial Revolution and Beyond:

- 19th Century: The Industrial Revolution brought about massive societal changes. The stark contrast between the wealthy and the working poor led to movements like socialism and anarchism, which were distinctly community-focused, advocating for workers' rights, equality, and communal ownership.

- Early 20th Century: With the rise of labour unions, suffragette movements, and socialist parties, there was a clear shift. The Russian Revolution of 1917 marked a significant moment where community governance and economic equality were attempted on a national scale.

Post-War and Cold War:

- 1940s-1980s: The aftermath of World War II and the Cold War era saw the spread of welfare states in the

West, influenced by socialist ideals but tempered with capitalism. This was a period where community welfare, public health, and education became government responsibilities, aligning with left-wing values.

- 1960s-70s: The counterculture movements, civil rights movements, and anti-war protests furthered left-wing community activism, focusing on civil liberties, racial equality, and peace, often challenging established norms from a community solidarity standpoint.

Late 20th Century to Present:

- 1980s-90s: The fall of the Soviet Union might have seemed a blow to leftist ideologies, but it also led to a redefinition. The Third Way in politics, like Blair's New Labour, tried blending traditional left values with market economics, emphasizing community but within a globalized capitalist framework.

- Globalization and Identity Politics: With globalization, traditional boundaries blurred, leading to new forms of solidarity and division. Identity politics gained prominence, where movements for racial, gender, and sexual equality became central, often supported by left-aligned ideologies.

- Digital Age and social media: The internet has been a double-edged sword. While it is allowed for global solidarity movements like #MeToo or Black Lives Matter, it is also fragmented discourse, where echo chambers can radicalize or moderate political views.

- New Left Movements: The 21st century has seen movements like Occupy Wall Street, highlighting economic inequality, or the youth-driven climate activism with figures like Greta Thunberg, blending environmentalism with left-wing economics.

- Electoral Shifts: The success of figures like Bernie Sanders or Jeremy Corbyn represents a revitalization of left-wing ideals, focusing on wealth redistribution, universal basic income, and climate justice.

Conclusion:

The evolution towards left-wing politics through community changes is not linear but reflects waves of reaction to economic conditions, technological changes, and social injustices.

From early communal living, through the intellectual ferment of the Enlightenment, the industrial struggles, to the digital activism of today, communities have continuously redefined what equality, justice, and governance should look like.

This evolution underscores those political ideologies, especially those on the left, are deeply interwoven with how societies organize, interact, and evolve over time, always pushing towards what its proponents see as a more just and equitable world.t

Chapter 5: The North Pole

Here I will say obvious things and perhaps rant about it. Firstly, I need to talk about path to understanding politics, even though this whole book had been about that but here we go.

Embracing Nuanced Views

Embracing nuanced views means looking at the world through a lens that is not just black or white, but filled with shades of grey. It is about seeing that life, politics, and society are complex, and solutions to problems often do not fit neatly into one ideological box.

Here is why adopting this mindset is crucial for anyone aiming to navigate the political landscape with a balanced perspective:

Nuanced thinking starts with acknowledging that humans are not one-dimensional. Each person comes with their own set of experiences, values, and information that shapes their beliefs.

This means that when we encounter someone with an opposing view, there is often more to their stance than we might initially perceive.

For instance, someone advocating for stricter immigration policies might do so out of a concern for national security or economic stability, not necessarily from a place of xenophobia.

By understanding this, we open the possibility of finding common ground where both security and humane immigration policies can coexist.

Moreover, nuanced views help us recognize that policies and ideologies have unintended consequences. A policy that seems perfect in theory might fail in practice due to unforeseen issues or because it overlooks certain societal needs. By considering multiple perspectives, we can anticipate these pitfalls better, leading to more effective solutions.

Take environmental policy, for example; while one might argue for complete bans on certain industries, a nuanced approach might consider how to transition workers, support alternative livelihoods, and phase out harmful practices without causing economic upheaval.

No Brainer on Critical Thinking

First off, critical thinking means we do not just accept what we are told. Imagine if every time someone said something, we believed it without question.

We would be filled with misinformation. Instead, we should ask questions like "How do they know this?" or "What evidence supports this claim?" This habit helps us sift through the flood of information we encounter daily, from social media to news reports, and choose what is likely to be true.

Secondly, it teaches us to look at problems from different angles. Think of it like solving a puzzle. If one piece does not fit, you do not throw it away in frustration; you try it from another angle.

Critical thinkers do this with problems or decisions. They consider various solutions, weigh the pros and cons, and think about the long-term effects.

This mindset is invaluable in making better decisions, whether it is choosing a career path, voting in an election, or solving a community issue.

Critical thinking also involves recognizing our biases. Everyone has them—those little voices in our heads that make us lean one way or another without real thought.

By acknowledging these biases, we can step back and try to see things more objectively. It is like being your own referee in a game where you are both a player and coach, ensuring fair play.

Moreover, it encourages us to connect the dots. Information does not exist in isolation. Understanding how history, science, culture, and personal experiences intersect can give us a deeper insight into why things are the way they are.

This interconnected thinking helps us understand complex issues, from climate change to economic crises, not as separate facts but as parts of a larger, more intricate tapestry.

Lastly, critical thinking fosters open-mindedness and empathy. When you are used to questioning your own beliefs and understanding how you came by them, it becomes easier to understand why others think differently.

This does not mean you will agree with everyone, but you will be better equipped to engage in meaningful dialogue, see where they are coming from, and perhaps find common ground or areas for mutual growth.

In essence, critical thinking is not just a skill for academics or philosophers. It is a life skill that makes us better at everything we do—better learners, better problem solvers, better citizens, and better humans.

By practicing this skill daily, we not only improve our own lives but also contribute to a more informed, thoughtful, and compassionate society.

Respectful Discourse: Imagine you are at a dinner table with family or friends. Everyone has different views on topics like politics, sports, or even what movie to watch next. If everyone shouts over each other, no one gets heard, and the evening ends in frustration.

But if everyone listens and speaks their turn, even when disagreeing, the conversation can be enriching. This is the essence of respectful discourse. It is about treating others' opinions with the same respect you would like for your own. It means listening not just to reply but to understand.

When we engage in respectful discourse, we are not trying to win a fight but to learn from each other.

This approach opens minds, fosters empathy, and can lead to solutions that would not have been considered if everyone was stuck in their own corner.

Avoiding Echo Chambers: Think of an echo chamber like a room where the walls only bounce back your own voice.

You talk, and all you hear is what you just said, louder. In the world of information, this happens when we only consume news or opinions that align with our own beliefs.

Social media feeds, news subscriptions, or even the friends we choose can create this echo.

The danger here is that we start believing our views are universally accepted because we never hear anything different.

Supporting Bipartisan Efforts

Being vocal about something important is more important than being silent for something important.

Supporting bipartisan efforts means backing initiatives where both major political parties come together to find common ground. It is about recognizing that despite our differences, there are shared goals that can benefit everyone.

Here is why putting our weight behind these efforts is crucial:

Firstly, bipartisanship helps in passing legislation that might otherwise be stuck in partisan gridlock.

When both sides agree, laws and policies can move forward quicker, leading to faster changes and solutions that address pressing issues.

This approach can tackle big challenges like infrastructure development, healthcare reforms, or even tackling climate change, where broad agreement can lead to more comprehensive and effective policies.

Moreover, bipartisan efforts restore some faith in government. When people see their elected officials from different parties working together, it sends a message that government can function for the good of all, not just along party lines.

This reduces cynicism and increase civic engagement, as citizens might feel more inclined to participate if they believe their government represents a wider consensus rather than just one side of the political spectrum.

Not to mention a lot of people confuse skepticism with cynicism!

Economically, supporting bipartisan initiatives often leads to more stable and beneficial outcomes for businesses and the economy at large.

For instance, when tax policies or infrastructure projects gain bipartisan support, they're less likely to be overturned by the next administration, providing long-term predictability that businesses crave. This stability encourages investment, job creation, and economic growth.

On a social level, bipartisan efforts can foster a sense of unity. Politics can be divisive, but when leaders from different backgrounds agree on certain issues, it can set an example for the public.

It shows that despite our differences, there are fundamental values and goals that we all share, like wanting safe communities, good education, or economic prosperity.

This can bridge social divides, making society feel more cohesive.

Environmentally, bipartisan support can lead to more robust environmental policies. Climate change, for example, affects everyone, and solutions require all hands on deck.

When both parties endorse environmental legislation, it not only strengthens the laws but also ensures they're more likely to be enforced over time, providing consistency in environmental efforts which ecosystems desperately need.

Economic Pragmatism

Now, there's one thing about politicians hating or coallating with each other, but it affects economics at broad and people get affected in the ceasefire.

Now, Economic pragmatism is about using common sense when making decisions about money, jobs, and how we run our country's finances.

Instead of sticking to one set of rules or theories, it's about finding what works best at any given time. Here's why this approach matters:

Imagine you're planning a family budget. You want to save for the future, but you also need to spend on things like food and education right now.

You might decide to cut back on unnecessary spending, invest in ways that could pay off later, and maybe even borrow a little if it means you can build something valuable, like a home or education. This mix of saving, spending, and investing is economic pragmatism on a personal scale.

On a national level, it means governments should look at what's happening in the economy at that moment.

If the economy is struggling, maybe it's time to spend more to get things moving again, like building infrastructure or giving people tax breaks to spend more.

But if the economy is booming, it might be wise to save or reduce spending to prepare for tougher times ahead or to prevent inflation from getting out of control.

That's about it. If you embibe all that's written, you become a *political constant*. Thanks for reading the book!

www.ingramcontent.com/pod-product-compliance
Lightning Source LLC
Chambersburg PA
CBHW031320130726
47988CB00007B/2907